With love for Anna Bugg, who inspired us all.

First edition for the United States, its dependencies, the
Philippine Islands, and Canada published in 2016 by
Barron's Educational Series, Inc.

Copyright © Frances Lincoln 2016
Text and illustrations © 2016 by Laurence Anholt
Frida Kahlo and the Bravest Girl in the World was conceived,
edited, and produced by Frances Lincoln Limited, a subsidiary
of Quarto Publishing Plc of The Old Brewery, 6 Bundell Street,
London N7 9BH, England

All inquiries should be addressed to:
Barron's Educational Series, Inc.
250 Wireless Boulevard
Hauppauge, New York 11788
www.barronseduc.com

ISBN: 978-0-7641-6837-6

Library of Congress Control Number: 2016930185

Product conforms to all applicable CPSC and CPSIA 2008
standards. No lead or phthalate hazards.

Manufactured by: RR Donnelly, Dongguan, Guangdong, China
Date of Manufacture: June 2016

Printed in China
9 8 7 6 5 4 3 2 1

Photographic Acknowledgments

Please note: the pages in this book are not numbered. The story
begins on page 6.

Paintings by Frida Kahlo © 2015.
Banco de México Diego Rivera Frida Kahlo Museums Trust,
Mexico, D.F./DACS.

Page 7 above left: Portrait of Engineer Eduardo Morillo Safa,
1944, Fundacion Dolores Olmedo, Mexico City. © 2015 Photo
SCALA, Florence

Page 7 above right: Portrait of Lupita Morillo Safa, 1944,
Private Collection

Page 7 below: Portrait of Alicia Morillo Safa and her son
Eduardo, 1944, Mexico City. © 2015 Photo SCALA, Florence

Page 8: Portrait of Doña Rosita Morillo, 1944, Fundacion Dolores
Olmedo, Mexico City. © 2015 Photo SCALA, Florence

Page 13: Frida Kahlo: Self-Portrait with Monkeys, 1943.
Photo: akg-images

Page 30: Portrait of Mariana Morillo Safa, 1944,
Private Collection

Page 31: Photograph of Frida Kahlo in San Francisco, 1939.
Photo: akg-images

Frida Kahlo

and the Bravest Girl in the World

LAURENCE ANHOLT

There was once a girl with big brown eyes. Her name was Mariana.

She lived in a house in Mexico, full of paintings by a famous artist named Frida Kahlo.

Frida had painted Mariana's daddy.

Frida had painted her big sister, Lupita.

Frida had painted her mom and her brother, Eduardo.

But Mariana's favorite painting was of her wise granny, Dona Rosita. Frida Kahlo had painted every white hair on her grandma's head, so the painting seemed almost alive.

"I want to be painted too!" said Mariana.

"You are too little," said her big sister.

"You could never sit still, Mariana," said Dona Rosita. "Frida made me sit for so long I knitted three scarves and a sweater."

"Anyway, Mariana would be scared to go to Frida's house," teased her brother. "It's full of strange paintings and **Frida keeps a skeleton above her bed.**"

Mariana's eyes grew big and wide.

But one day Mariana's daddy said, "Mariana, now it is your turn. You can go to Frida's house on Saturday."

Mariana felt very nervous as she rang the bell at the Blue House.

She waited a long time.

She thought about the strange paintings and the skeleton.

At last the door opened and there stood Frida Kahlo....

She was as beautiful as a Mexican princess!

Frida wore rings on her fingers
and flowers in her hair,
and a beautiful dress
which reached right to the floor.

"Hello, Mariana," said Frida.
"How are you doing?"

"I'm a little scared,"
said Mariana.

"Well, that's
OK," said Frida.
"Everyone feels
scared sometimes.
Now take my hand
and let's go inside."

If Frida was a
princess, her house was
like a bright blue
fairy-tale palace.

Frida did not have children, but she had lots of animals.
"Come and meet my friends," she said.

"This is Fulang Chang, my spider monkey.

This is Bonito, my parrot.

This is my favorite little dog.
He's called Mr. Xoloti."

"What a funny name!" said Mariana.

"This is my baby deer, Granizo.

And this is my beautiful eagle,
Gertrude Caca Blanca."

"What does Gertrude Caca Blanca mean?"
asked Mariana.

"Hey, kiddo," laughed Frida.
"Don't you know?
It means Gertrude White Poo!"

Mariana almost laughed.
But she was still a little frightened.

"Listen, Little Sister," whispered Frida.
"If you are very lucky you will meet my favorite friend of all.
He's an ugly frog-toad, **as big as an elephant.**"

Mariana's eyes grew big and wide.
She knew that princesses liked frogs. But she
hoped she wouldn't have to kiss him.

"You and I are going to be pals," said Frida.
"Let's go to my studio."

Frida walked very slowly, with a
stick in one hand. They went into
the studio filled with Frida's
paintings—the pictures were
strange but they were
very beautiful.

"OK, now, let's get to work," said Frida.

Mariana sat in a tall chair.
Her feet didn't even touch the ground.

Mariana tried to sit still.
She looked at all the funny
things in the studio—toys and
candy and dolls.

"Frida, where is the enormous frog-toad?" she asked.

"Oh, he'll hop along at lunchtime," said Frida.
"My frog-toad is always hungry."

They sat in the sunshine and ate delicious food.
Mariana gave a banana to Fulang Chang. Frida gave
some apple to Granizo.

Then the gate opened and someone came
into the yard.

All of a sudden, Mariana felt scared.
She saw an enormous man with a
fat tummy and **big froggy eyes.**

Frida gave the man a kiss. "Mariana, meet Diego, my favorite frog-toad. Diego, this is my friend, Mariana. I'm painting her today."

Diego smiled and kissed Mariana's hand. Then he ate the biggest meal that Mariana had ever seen.

"Diego is a great painter," said Frida. "Maybe the greatest painter in Mexico."

"And my Frida is **the greatest painter in the world,**" said Diego.

After lunch Frida said, "I'm too tired to paint any more. I need to rest a while. Help me to my bedroom, Little Sister."

Mariana remembered what her brother had said.

"I think I'll go home now," she said.
"I don't like skeletons."

"You're funny!"
laughed Frida.

There was Frida's bed and on top of the bed was—**the skeleton.**

But this skeleton was not scary at all!

It was a big toy skeleton with a funny hat and a silly smile on its face.

Frida rested while Mariana looked at the colorful clothes in her wardrobe.

"I love your dresses," she said.
"Thanks," said Frida.
"You know why I wear a long dress all the time?"

"Because you are a princess," said Mariana.

Frida laughed. "Listen, Little Sister, come and sit beside me
and I'll tell you a true story...

...When I was a young girl I went to school in the city.

One day I got on a bus with a boy..."

"Was he your boyfriend?" asked Mariana.

"Yes, he was my boyfriend," laughed Frida.

"Anyway, a dreadful thing happened. The bus was in a crash with a tram.

It was a terrible accident. They put me in the hospital for a long, long time."

"Poor Frida. Did it hurt?"

"It did hurt. It hurt me then and it hurts me now.
It hurt so bad they had to make a special plaster coat to hold
my body still. They carried me home and put me in this bed.
I was dead scared, Little Sister.
I thought my life was over."

"But it wasn't over, was it, Frida?"

"No way, kiddo. I was just beginning. One day my papa
made me a special easel and gave me some paints.

He even fixed a mirror above my bed. 'Look up
there, Frida,' he said. 'That's the bravest girl
in the world.'"

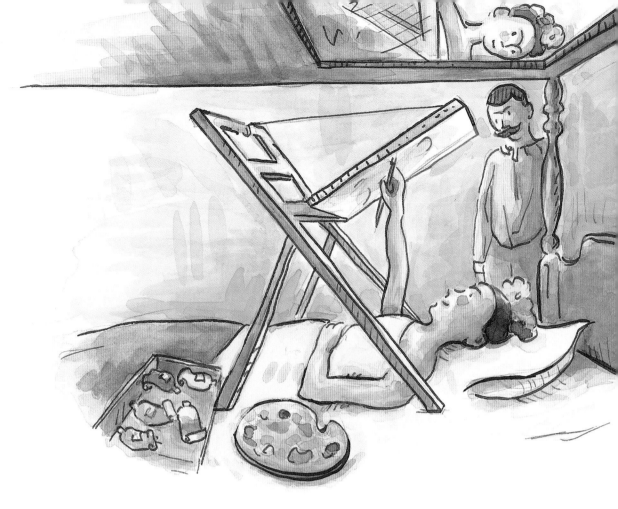

"And that's when you started painting!"

"You've got it. I said to the funny skeleton, 'Listen, Boney,
Frida may be broken, but she sure isn't finished. I'm never
going to be scared of anything again. I'm going to be a painter.
I'm going to be a better painter than any man in Mexico!'"

"And if it wasn't for the accident, you
wouldn't be an artist!" said Mariana.

"Maybe that's true. The doctors told me I would never walk again,
but **no one** tells Frida what to do! Slowly I learned to walk, but I
always wore long dresses to cover my broken leg."

All week Mariana waited for Saturday so she could go back to the Blue House.

Mariana loved Frida and Frida loved Mariana.
She told her lots of funny things to make her laugh.

"Look here, Little Sister. Have you ever seen anything like it?"

Hanging on the line were three pairs of pink
underpants, big enough for an elephant.

"They belong to Diego!" giggled Frida.
"He's so big, he has them specially made!"

But sometimes Frida had to paint in a wheelchair.

Mariana felt very sad for Frida. But Frida said,

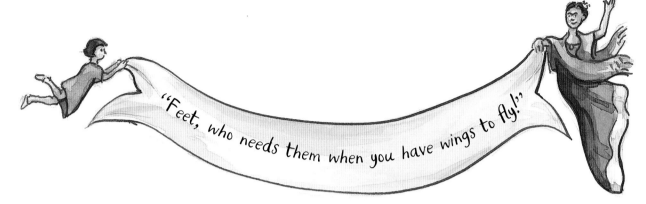

"Feet, who needs them when you have wings to fly!"

"We are stronger than we think, Mariana. And here's a little secret—
women are stronger than men.

It's true!

Diego is a huge enormous frog-toad, but he's really
like a big baby. Did I tell you that he plays with
toys in his bath? I am only small, Little Sister,
and I suffer all the time, but in my heart
I am stronger than any man alive."

Frida gave Mariana lots of presents—a special little chair so that
Mariana's feet could reach the ground. And her own baby skeleton with a
hat. Mariana looked at the skeleton and she said, "Listen, Boney. I'm the
bravest girl in the world."

Then one Saturday, Frida said
the painting was finished.

"Let me see! Let me see!"
called Mariana.

Frida only smiled.

She wrapped the painting in brown paper and tied a ribbon around it.
She told Mariana to open it at home.

"Your granny, Dona Rosita, is a wise old woman.
If she likes the painting, then it can't be too bad. But listen, Mariana—
I have painted a name at the bottom of the picture.
It is the name of the **strongest,**
bravest,
most beautiful little woman I know."

"Of course," said Mariana, "You have signed your name—
FRIDA—on the painting. No one is braver than you."

Mariana said goodbye to the animals.

And when she kissed Diego, the big frog-toad, she pretended
she didn't know about his pink underpants or his bath toys.

Frida had one last present for Mariana—
a Mexican princess dress, just like hers!

"Promise me you'll be strong like me, Little Sister.
Promise me you will fly in your life."

Mariana kissed Frida and hugged her hard and promised that she would.
Then she took her daddy's hand and walked out of the Blue House.

"Well," said Granny Dona Rosita.

"Can we see your painting?"

Everybody gathered around as Mariana untied the ribbon.

There was the girl with the big brown eyes, sitting perfectly still on her own special chair.

Dona Rosita said it was the most beautiful painting in Mexico. And she should know—she's a very wise old lady.

And underneath was the name of the
strongest, bravest girl in the world.